I0559794

Life of Anxiously Attached Couples

35+ Activities to Characterize Your Connection Style, and Understand Your Partner by Building Strong and Secure Relationship

By

Brenda R.

Serene Publications

About the Author

Brenda R. is a well-known psychologist. Years of working with individuals and couples in the clinical setting have given her a thorough grasp of the difficulties faced by people with anxious attachment styles. She has written extensively, drawing on their knowledge and kind demeanor to offer insightful analysis and viable tactics for reducing anxiety and fostering healthier relationships. Because of her vast knowledge and experience, Life of Anxiously Attached Couples provides readers with a transformational and perceptive investigation of anxious attachment in partnerships.

Table of Contents

What if you could identify what prevents you from having satisfying relationships? You may have been with your partner, yet you still battle with the idea that they will never be able to satisfy your needs completely. Many people think that they will never find true love. They frequently worry that once they reveal "the real me," their partners will leave. They occasionally think that their partners are appreciative of what they do. But more is needed. What if it deteriorates?

This book will help you confront these difficulties.

The warmth, acceptance, and assurance provided by your parents or other people who cared for you served as the foundation for your initial growth. You honed a particular way of attaching to others over the first few years and months of your life.

It is vital to realize that attachment-related anxiety does not necessarily result from parenting that is visibly abusive or destructive; in fact, this is not the case the majority of the time. Many persons who experience anxiety connected to attachment have grown up in loving environments. Even though their parents genuinely loved their children, their problems or challenging or traumatic situations prevented them from being effective parents.

Increasing self-awareness is a crucial factor in encouraging personal progress. This entails being aware of your thoughts, accepting and fully experiencing your emotions. Such self-awareness typically makes people feel better and frequently enables change, such as lowering anxiety connected to attachment and fostering stronger relationships.

This book helps you understand how your relationship difficulties began, what makes change so difficult, and how to overcome those challenges to find a solid, lasting love.

This book teaches you to break the shackles of an anxious attachment, but you can also learn more about your partner by using the concepts I present. To relate to your partner with greater compassion and foster a stronger relationship, you may sometimes need a window into their world.

Mark up the margins with notes. Reread any essential passages, and if necessary, pause in one to work on putting it into practice before going on. Give exercises time as opposed to rushing through them. Please keep a journal to reply to the activities, elaborate on your ideas, and reflect on them afterward.

Best of luck!

Chapter 1: The Basics of Our Connections

When you are unfortunate, who do you turn to? Your attachment mechanism is activated at specific times, similar to activating an internal homing device whose destination or "home" is your attachment figure or a connection you are close to. When an adult's attachment system functions properly, it gives birth to a secure attachment style. When sad, he turns to his partner or another prominent attachment figure for consolation. Once he determines that his attachment figure is consistently accessible, he is at ease.

Yet, those with an irregular attachment pattern have a conflicting relationship with themselves and the people around them. In this chapter, we will see how our early connections shape our attachment style, the types of attachment styles, and why it is crucial to know your attachment style.

1.1 Our Early Connections

Witnessing a birth is like seeing a miracle. No mother can help but want to cradle, smother, and care for her newborn. And this is how the story of every person's relationship starts.

To survive, infants depend on their parents. So, there is a yearning to connect with others and the means to achieve it. For instance, they enjoy staring at people's faces and can elicit compassion from others by sobbing. Naturally, people want to care for newborns because they are so cute. This maintains their primary caretakers' interest in preserving and nourishing them, typically their moms and, secondarily, their fathers.

Children are driven to remain near their mothers as they grow mobile because of their ongoing need for assistance to survive. From infancy, people learn how relationships can protect and calm them.

The attachment system is a survival mechanism provided by nature, yet the relationships formed within it are perceived as love in both childhood and maturity. Thus, it is no surprise that kids cling to their parents' love as their existence depends on it. When the continuation of their key relationships (and the love such partnerships bring) feels threatened, adults similarly suffer the acute worry and excruciating despair. It is also not surprising that individuals, who struggle to manage their emotions as children, have problems struggling to control their emotions as adults and find a constant, reliable sense of soothing and safety in romantic partnerships. It is all connected.

1.2 Types of Attachment Styles

The easiest approach to comprehending attachment styles is to combine how people relate to themselves (which can cause anxiety) and to an attachment figure (which can cause avoidance). You can use this book better if you recognize the "blurriness" of these types. It will make you evaluate your attachment style and put yourself in a box. You wouldn't be considering everything that makes you — the unique individual that you are — who you are. The best strategy to develop yourself and lessen relationship anxiety is mainly based on self-awareness.

Hence, rather than just focusing on which group you fall into when reading about these styles, consider how much you relate to each one.

Take Linda, for instance. She had an anxious attachment style and had always felt insufficient. Her husband's constant attention to her flaws and errors furthered this impression. With their final divorce, she struggled with a stronger sense of being unlovable. Yet as she received therapy, she started to doubt her negative self-perception. Her husband had been unduly critical. She then met another person who appreciated her inventiveness and intelligence.

He pampered her, which softened the self-rejection that was still present and made her feel more at ease with someone else's appreciation. This book can assist you in realizing the unique potential that romantic relationships have for you to improve your attachment style and become healthier.

Moving toward a more secure manner is a crucial (though not the only) strategy to discover satisfaction when you are dissatisfied. But it is crucial to retain your focus on love as you assess your life and consider what needs to be altered.

There are four possible types of attachment styles. Let's discuss them one by one.

Secure Attachment Style

Susan was often a cheerful individual. She considered herself an excellent primary school teacher and loved what she did. She liked to go trekking and play tennis when she had free time. In addition, she was happily married. Of course, no romantic relationship is flawless. For instance, once, her husband forgot to take her out to dinner. Even in those circumstances, though, when she was upset, she believed that he genuinely cared for her.

Susan had a secure attachment.

In general, persons who feel secure in their attachment are at ease with their emotions and believe themselves to be admirable, moral, compassionate, and capable. Also, they tend to view their partners as emotionally supportive, trustworthy, sensitive, and well-intentioned. They are content with who they are and the people in their lives.

Securely attached people are content with their sexual life too. Because they place a great value on emotional closeness. They frequently stay faithful, feel at ease discussing sex, and delight in everything it offers.

This solid and healthy manner of relating will reassure you if you have an anxious attachment to having a securely connected spouse, allowing you to cultivate a more secure attachment style.

Anxious Attachment Style

> *Meet Jack, someone with whom you can have some similarity. He used to go to his lover Amy to tell her that he deserved love. But, he was unsure of what to think when she displayed interest in him because it contradicted how he saw himself.*
>
> *He was often concerned with how much Amy cared for him. He was confident that as soon as she discovered "the real him," she would leave him immediately. He assumed she was ignoring him anytime she did not reply to his messages immediately. He was consumed by the enormous fear of being rejected, which was a real possibility.*

Individuals with an Anxious attachment style, like Jack, are concerned about being ignored or rejected by their partner, who protects them. They employ hyperactivating methods, guaranteeing that they will remain to look for a trustworthy attachment figure. They can overreact and underestimate their capacity to handle their relationships. They intensify their desire for an attachment figure by producing all these unfavorable emotions and ideas. Sadly, people who take it too far may develop a persistent sense of helplessness and being overwhelmed.

Unintentionally, any potential symptoms of rejection lead to arguments and distancing in their close relationships. They will react with worry when their partners misunderstand them, are physically unavailable, or do not respond in a loving enough manner. Anxious individuals can start new love, but they frequently quickly become entangled in their suffering. When this happens, people are more likely to perceive their partners as unloving (or not constantly available), unreliable, and possible infidelity.

They become too possessive and jealous as a result. Even worse, they frequently find it difficult to control their emotions and forgive their spouses for transgression. Some persons with an anxious attachment style plan their life around attempting to demonstrate their deservingness of love or detach themselves from their unpleasant feelings since their attachment demands and struggles feel so powerful. This hampers their capacity to engage in their own interests or authentic self-expression.

People with an anxious attachment style turn to sex to obtain the confidence and acceptance they desire, even if they frequently enjoy having more profound physical closeness. Males tend to be more sexually reserved and seek partners who are sexually receptive and satisfied to feel loved. In contrast, women prefer to be less reserved or even promiscuous to feel loved by a man.

This book aims to help these kinds of anxious couples.

Avoidant Attachment Style

> *Meet Bob now. Consider whether you can relate to him in any way or if he reminds you of someone you know. He took pride in his self-reliance, independence, and dedication to his work as a salesperson.*
>
> *He liked hanging out with his ex-girlfriend but wasn't too sad when she broke things up. She wanted him to phone her during his work trips, but she just requested an occasional check-in, which seemed to him to be making a huge deal out of nothing.*
>
> *Additionally, he thought she wanted to talk "all the time" about her emotions and their relationship. He was relieved that he no longer needed to care for her. He claimed that even though he occasionally felt excluded when his buddies were chatting about their partners, he was not upset and preferred to be alone. Even to himself, Bob tried to hide the fact that he consciously downplayed and avoided his emotions.*

Like people with an anxious approach, dismissive/avoidant individuals are prone to think that their partners won't consistently be available to console or support them. However, individuals defend themselves by unwittingly employing deactivation techniques that "switch off" (or deactivate) their attachment system. It makes them uncomfortable to feel drawn to rely on an unreliable partner. They successfully repress, deny, or dismiss their attachment demands and emotions. They routinely disparage their partners, maintain a distance, and restrict their encounters and private chats.

Avoidant persons frequently lack emotional awareness and are ill-prepared to handle emotionally distressing situations. For instance, they attempt to downplay or suppress their anger when their spouses irritate them. Nonetheless, they frequently become tense and unforgiving due to underlying hatred. Naturally, this feature is unsuitable for their relationships, but because so much of it happens with their knowledge, it is easier to discuss or change. The anxiously attached partners who tend to read the avoidant partner's rage find this dynamic the most difficult.

Then why does not the partner leave the avoidance even they need companionship? As a result, they seek out and maintain romantic relationships while defending their interests by being overly independent.

Avoidant people handle their sexuality in a similarly cold, self-contained manner in which they view relationships in general. In close relationships, they are less likely to show affection and exhibit emotional disengagement while having sex. As a result, their spouses may feel unattractive and unlovable.

Fearful-Avoidant Attachment Style

William took care of himself by the time he was fourteen because his mother was busy trying to keep the long working hours, and his father was an alcoholic. He viewed himself as imperfect, dependent, defenseless, and unlovable. And he thought people avoided him because they suspected something was wrong with him. Thus, even though he would adore a severe and passionate relationship, he stayed far out of concern that he would be turned away from or misinterpreted.

People with a Fearful-avoidant attachment style frequently experience this struggle between an intense dread of connection and a pressing desire for confirmation and connection. When they do not entirely avoid connections, they act inconsistently and incoherently. They frequently use hyperactivating techniques, such as showing distress, in a desperate attempt to get their lovers' favor and attention.

They are prone to view their relationships as emotionally aloof. Nonetheless, they feel exposed to harm when they sense a closeness developing between their partners. As a result, they naturally try to defend themselves against their spouse by activating avoidance mechanisms. Fearfully connected people become chronically agitated, insecure, incredibly passive, and emotionally aloof due to this ongoing tension.

Fearfully attached persons tend to perceive their relationships in a particularly negative light and have difficulty empathizing with them.

> *For instance, when Robert and Ana were dating, and they would meet for dinner after work, he would always assume she wasn't interested in him when, in fact, she was just exhausted from a hard day.*

Of course, this tendency causes conflict in partnerships. However, terrified people tend to suppress their emotions. They frequently stay in relationships, even when severely troublesome or abusive, probably because they believe they deserve love. On the other side, even when they are in love, and their partner is genuinely caring, they abandon a relationship because of their difficulty with closeness and being appreciated.

They struggle with physical intimacy with their spouses in the same way that they do with emotional intimacy. In some instances, this entails engaging in casual intercourse to satisfy the other person's needs for consolation, acceptance, and reassurance while maintaining emotional distance and safety. People might engage in one-night stands or casual liaisons for this. They are more prone to shun sexual closeness and the vulnerability that comes with it when they are less concerned with fulfilling their needs and more concerned with protecting themselves.

Importance of Knowing Your Connection Style

Consider the different attachment styles in addition to evaluating your style. Think about the communication methods of your present or former partners, as well as your friends and coworkers. Your fear of attachment may lead you to form erroneous emotional assessments of other people quickly. You also need to understand your partner's feelings, emotions, and actions. If you do not, this may lead to severe problems in your relationship.

You can better comprehend your partner and the complexities of your relationship if you are aware of their attachment style. A solid understanding of secure attachment will also enable you to appreciate the advantages of working toward it for yourself and the advantages of having a secure partner

If you haven't before, review the four attachment types and choose which one you closely resemble. However, remember that you won't perfectly fit any style. So, pay close attention to how elements of the other forms are incorporated into your distinctive attachment style. For instance, do you generally feel safe yet tend to question your value? In the next chapter, we will discuss this in more detail on how you can find your attachment style.

After you are confident of your own, consider your partner's attachment style. Using your observations of them and their behaviors, you can evaluate them as you evaluate yourself. You can ask your existing partner to rank yourself. This has the advantage of opening up enlightening and intimacy-enhancing talks.

You can comprehend your relationship better if you know their attachment style. And finally, the most effective way to change your attachment pattern is to become aware of it. Therefore, even just getting to this point was a huge accomplishment. It is also crucial to comprehend the development of your style.

And I will talk about this next.

Chapter 2: The World of Anxious Attachment Style

As we learned in chapter one, human relationships are fundamentally shaped by attachment, which determines how we establish and maintain ties with others. The attachment system is dynamic and complicated, affecting our ideas, feelings, and actions in interpersonal interactions. One of the significant attachment styles is anxious attachment, characterized by a heightened need for intimacy, a fear of abandonment, and a propensity to seek assurance from others. This chapter will explore the world of anxious attachment style and examine its causes, symptoms, and effects on romantic relationships.

2.1 The Functions of an Attachment System

Your attachment system has some fundamental purposes and functions. People naturally try to maintain a tight relationship with their attachment figure, typically their parent or love partner.

When people are in danger, they turn to attachment figures for safety, solace, and support. So, we need a safe and secure place. People are more willing to pursue goals outside of an attachment connection when supported by that person.

2.2 A Safe Place

Children are conditioned from birth to see their parents as a refuge from danger. Many young toddlers, for instance, flee to their parents for safety during thunderous storms or when they encounter a clown at the circus. However, more than providing physical security is required for parents. In the presence of their parents, children must feel secure and comforted.

The ideal parents are those who can keep their emotional balance. Their feelings do not consume them. These parents continue to give compassionate replies to help their kids accept, comprehend, and deal with their feelings.

Some kids need a trustworthy, safe place. They have not felt deserving of love and entirely accepted. Additionally, they have perceived their parents as emotionally distant and unsupportive. These encounters with oneself and others continue into maturity. Therefore, if your childhood caregivers were unreliable or incapable of giving you a compassionate relationship, you might be distracted by the worry that your spouse will leave you or decide not to even turn to you for solace.

You must face your anxieties of rejection and unlovability, comprehend them, and cultivate a new sense of safety with your partner to be in a stable and contented relationship. Although it is not a simple task, it can be done. Complete the following exercise to prepare you better to tackle and comprehend this problem.

Activity 1: Finding Your Sensitivity Level

Are you easily moved to feelings of abandonment, rejection, or uncaring? If so, permit yourself to feel, recognize, and investigate your feelings. (for example, feeling painfully alone or vulnerable).

Whatever your reactions, remember that they arise from an attachment system developed to protect you from harm. Your attachment system uses your strength of emotion as a signal that it needs assistance.

Here is what you need to do:

> - Think about a time when you and your partner were physically separated.
> - See how sensitive you were to separation.
> - Spend time reflecting on when you and your partner were apart, and write down your responses.

2.3 A Secure Base

Attachment figures offer refuge in times of need and give kids a safe foundation from which to build their experience. This is significant because everyone has an intrinsic urge to understand and control their surroundings.

When kids successfully receive this kind of support, they gradually grow more independent, gain a sense of autonomy, and can act on their intrinsic interests and values.

Children need to be appreciated for their identity to establish a solid foundation. They must learn about conflicts and divergent viewpoints. People lucky enough to have their parents as a reliable foundation grow to have great self-esteem and intense feeling. They are more inclined to pursue their hobbies, work hard, and succeed in school and the workplace. They typically feel linked to and supported by their partners in romantic relationships. Furthermore, they typically have positive relationships and are skilled at navigating social settings. But not everyone experiences this.

Reading about the advantages of a stable base may bring to light some of your significant challenges, such as a reluctance to express yourself to your spouse and a failure to pursue (or even identify) your hobbies and passions if you experience a moderate amount of attachment-related anxiety. Even though it is difficult to stress, you are already making progress simply by being aware of how having a safe basis would benefit you. I will point you toward strategies for enhancing your sense of security in both yourself and your relationships later in the book.

Activity 2: Knowing Your Attachment Style

Of course, relationships involve more dynamic balancing than maintaining a constant state of balance. Which of the following images best captures your ideal relationship in light of that?

Which image, if any, most accurately depicts your most recent or current relationship?

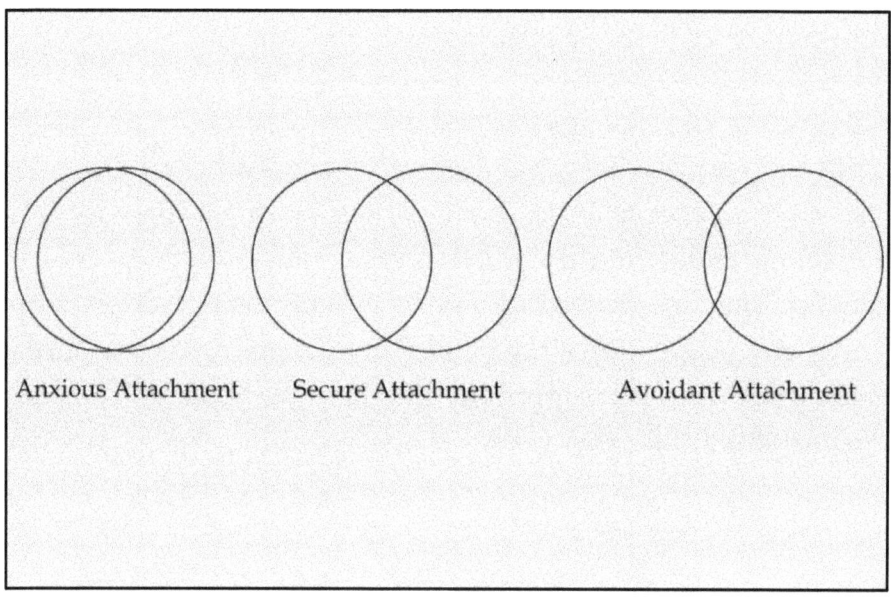

The following statements represent these styles:

Secure Style

**Mark the statements that apply to you and your
relationship with your partner.**

☐ I am fine doing activities and have fun without my partner.

☐ It feels safe to share my share life with my partner.

☐ I still feel loved by my partner even when we pursue interests away

from one another.

☐ Even when we disagree, my partner respects and honor my opinions.

☐ It is acceptable for both my partner and I to rely on one another.

Anxious Style

Mark the statements that apply to you and your relationship with your partner.

☐ I put my interests on the back burner in favor of what my spouse finds enjoyable.

☐ I give my partner's values and opinions precedence over my own.

☐ Whenever I see my partner growing distant, I feel compelled to reach out to them (for instance, by calling or messaging constantly), or I react furiously.

☐ Having my partner rely on me makes me uneasy.

Create sentences to represent your relationship better as you complete this task. (Since humans are complex, it is acceptable if your description contains sentences contradicting one another.)

Now think about how effectively your relationship satisfies your requirements for a:

Safe Place: How much do you rely on your partner to give you a sense of security, protection, and support during trying times?

Secure Base: How much does your partner encourage you to pursue your hobbies and objectives outside your romantic relationship? How effectively does your partnership help you feel confident in your authentic self?

2.4 Are You Overwhelmed in Your Relationships?

A child who experiences primitive panic has higher stress chemicals, cortisol and adrenaline. The "cuddle hormone," oxytocin, which fosters trust, safety, and connection, is also decreased simultaneously. A child protests, cries, or acts demandingly in response to his overwhelming feeling. He is essentially yelling for assistance. If his caretaker consistently fails to calm him, he will continue to be ready to resist and scream for assistance until he does.

These kids become adults in their most extreme forms, easily alarmed by the slightest indication of separation. They try to get their partner's attention by acting more distressed. (a hyperactivating strategy). However, even with a supporting spouse, their dread of rejection can prevent them from feeling at ease.

If you can in any way identify with this, you could also occasionally struggle to separate your feelings. Instead, you see them as an upsetting occurrence you can't even begin to discuss or deal with. You might resort to unhealthy habits like binge eating or using drugs as a coping mechanism.

People who struggle with attachment-related anxiety often also have other interpersonal issues that you may be able to identify with. For instance, you could avoid bringing up disagreements or issues with your relationship out of fear of rejection. Additionally, seeing the world (or your relationship) from your partner's perspective could be overwhelming. You can find it challenging to understand and support your relationship.

Fortunately, you may alter this if you occasionally feel overpowered by attachment-related worry. Additionally, choosing a more stable partner — someone who can console you — may ease your distress. For now, let's understand the world of our attachment system.

Activity 3: What are Your Boundaries?

You will be able to appreciate why you operate in the way you do now to a greater extent if you have a deeper understanding of how your coping techniques evolved. Throughout this practice, be kind to yourself. It is possible to develop a more profound sense of self in this area. Therefore, you should come back to this over and over.

You should seek comments from individuals familiar to you and whom you trust. This activity will help you understand where you should have boundaries in your relationships.

Amy's previous two lovers complained about her overwhelmed behavior. She grumbled that none of them showed much affection, but she also recognized their validity. She would repeatedly phone and contact them to get reassurance that they were still interested since she was continuously worried they would break up with her. She understood that this situation made her feel similar to how she had felt when her father passed away. She was wary of developing close relationships because she was worried they would reject her.

Take notes about where Amy should have boundaries in her relationship, and discuss this activity with close friends and family. But also take a break from it and then return to it when you've had a chance to develop personally and are more receptive to fresh ideas.

Activity 4: Identifying Your Anxious Pattern

Answer the following questions to acquire some insight into your anxious patterns. Consider it about a former partner if you do not now have a partner. Considering how these questions relate to your prior romantic relationships, you can also find it helpful to spot and emphasize a trend.

Do you worry that your partner will leave you, or do you frequently sense that they are emotionally distant? Do you immediately panic when you have this notion, feeling crushed and compelled to cling to your partner?

Can you see how you object to being left alone even if you aren't aware of it? Which examples would you give?

Do you frequently experience feelings of helplessness, incapacity, or defect?

How does your fear of being rejected negatively affect your relationship, such as causing issues with trust and making it harder for you to unwind and enjoy your partner's company? Does this happen on purpose or unintentionally?

Activity 5: Assess Your Attachment Style

Assess Your Anxiety

Determine your anxious attachment style and assess how much anxiety you have in your relationship. Give a rating to the following on a scale of 1 to 10. A higher rating indicates higher attachment-related anxiety.

"It means the world to me that my spouse and I are entirely emotionally connected. However, others do not desire to be as near to them as I do. I doubt myself and worry that I am not as good as him in our relationship. I am constantly concerned that he does not value my relationship with him as highly as I do. And I constantly wonder if my spouse truly loves me or if they would leave me."

Your Rating:

Chapter 3: Know Your Partner

I find it amazing when partners in a relationship feel like they don't know each other. They are largely unaware of what makes the other person tick. However, not everyone reacts in a relationship the same way. Individual differences exist in the distribution of power within groups. In reality, you and your partner may have distinct interactions due to the differences in your brains.

As a result, we each approach the table with a particular relationship style in mind. Occasionally, we may identify our partner's style.

Unhappy spouses frequently assert their ignorance and continue to do so throughout the relationship. This chapter looks at the causes of this mystification and suggests ways to deal with it in a relationship by knowing yourself and your partner.

3.1 How do We Relate to Others?

Everyone has a communication style that is consistent throughout time. How our parents or other primitive caregivers interacted with us as children set the bar by which we learned to adjust. Even though we are intelligent and exposed to new ideas, this circuitry stays the same as we mature. I don't mean to seem judgmental; it is a fact of biology and human nature.

Most couples enter into relationships utterly unaware of how they interact with others in a committed couple setting. They try to present themselves in the best possible way. It wouldn't make sense for someone to admit on a first date that they still spend much time alone. In the early stages of a relationship, couples may convey hints about their fundamental preferences for close contact, emotional intimacy, and worries about safety and security. But these tendencies start manifesting if one or both participants view the relationship as permanent.

We often act automatically and without much thought. Early childhood influences how our brains are wired to respond to physical proximity and duration of proximity. We must know this fundamental aspect of our encounters since we primarily run on autopilot. Furthermore, when courting, as opposed to when a relationship is more committed, we behave differently when physically close. For instance, many couples frequently touch while just starting, but this frequency drastically decreases after they start dating seriously.

Playfulness, interactivity, flexibility, and sensitivity define a secure connection. Positive emotions predominate because negative emotions are quickly subdued. In addition to relief, comfort, and shelter, we might anticipate fun, excitement, and novelty. When we have a strong foundation as children, we continue that foundation into adulthood. As I term it, we become a pillar.

We may have had several varying caregivers, but none was consistently dependable or available. Relationships can be replaced by almost anything, often unintentionally. A child's sense of security may be hampered by a caregiver's mental or physical sickness, unresolved loss, immaturity, and similar factors. If this occurs, we enter partnerships as adults with an underlying insecurity. That may cause us to isolate ourselves and avoid making many new friends.

So, there are three ways we relate to others. We can have a secure attachment and be a pillar, insecure avoidance, and insecure ambivalence. Let's discuss these three forms of relationships one by one. Most of us would like to feel secure if given a choice. But every one of us brings a unique perspective to the table. If things were same, think of how boring the world would be. I'd want to start by describing the benefits of each category to keep this in focus.

3.2 Secure Attachment

Natasha and James both entered the partnership with a sense of personal security. These pairings frequently led to the other spouse being more of a pillar. Because they had early caretakers who highly valued relationships and interactions, Natasha and James could serve as pillars for each other. Their parents were aware of and attentive to their communication attempts.

Natasha and James recalled receiving hugs, kisses, and rocking as babies. They remembered noticing a tender glint in their parents' eyes that they understood was explicitly reserved for them. They did not think the other was unduly dependent on them or clanged to them. And neither was concerned about moving too close or far apart.

When they were away for a while, they frequently communicated via phone and email with vivacity and good humor. Whether they were together or apart, they were not afraid to fully express their thoughts without worrying about the repercussions. Through these interactions, they developed a shared respect for their relationship bubble and saw themselves as guardians of their shared sense of security. They both had taken the time to get to know each other and created what essentially amounted to a manual containing all this information.

Because of their tenacity, compassion, and intricacy, this kind of relationship frequently attracts other people. They can quickly adjust to the demands of the situation. They are capable of making choices and living with the results.

They take care of their connections and selves. They will only bother with risky or unrewarding relationships since they want committed relationships. They are not scared to own their mistakes and are fast to fix any harm or misconceptions that may have occurred. They can manage to be together and be apart from their partner easily. They are adept at handling relationship difficulties.

Activity 6: Are You a Pillar?

Where Do You Stand?

Would you or your partner stand strong? Check this list to
see whether any of it relates to you before giving it to your
partner.

☐ I am okay by myself, but I also like being in a committed relationship.

☐ I like how my loved one will do anything to keep our relationship going.

☐ People tend to love me because I love people.

☐ My close relationships are important to me.

☐ My loved ones interrupting me does not bother me.

☐ I do not mind being touched and loved a lot.

3.3 Insecure Avoidance

Anne put off getting married because she believed her work would take up too much of her time. But after that, she met Charles, who seemed to share her values. After their wedding, they constructed a house with separate sections for him and her. They both created a workspace where they could work quietly. Early in their marriage, Anne and Charles decided against having children. They decided to have lots of travel and adventure.

Problems started soon. Anne began to lose interest in having sex. Charles was used to expect Anne making the first move, but she started to ignore his advances as she ceased making her own. Charles was the first to express loneliness, although his actions weren't all that different from hers.

Anne was not actively attempting to destroy her marriage. Instead, she was acting by what she knew from her experience. Anne was continuing the patterns that had existed at a very young age.

Being the lone child, Anne's parents, who both worked as professionals, hired a nanny to look after their daughter. Anne viewed her mother as intelligent but not overly sentimental. Anne was troubled by her inability to recollect any loving events.

In a word, Anne developed insecure avoidance due to her experiences. Anne discovered it was better to avoid looking at people for affection after observing how little her mother sought out physical contact. She concentrated on caring for herself instead. She had no trouble relating to other adults as a single adult.

But when Anne married Charles, he turned into the house she grew up in. She did not anticipate having frequent sexually intimate encounters

> *with him. His attempts to get her attention frequently came off as abrupt. She usually refused to engage with him unless he persuaded her to do so. If she was left alone for a short while, she lost herself in her own little world again.*
>
> *She was unaware that her urge to connect and depend on people, who were unresponsive, dismissive, and callous, as a child caused it.*

Unlike secure attachment, insecure avoidance typically faces higher levels of interpersonal stress. This is because they feel more threatened around their significant others and in social settings in general. They may worry that their need for remoteness may bring about tragedy.

These couples tend to look ahead and avoid reflecting on current interpersonal difficulties or previous relationships, including those from their formative years. Their catchphrase is "That's the past," which implies that recapping the past would be useless. In actuality, they cannot recall elements of their past and either idealize or hate it. When questioned about specifics, responses like "I don't remember," "It doesn't matter," "Who cares?" and similar ones are frequently used. The opposite partner may find this inclination to be very annoying.

Activity 7: Are You Better Alone?

Am I Better Alone?

Here are some statements that define an avoidant who feels insecure. Check to discover if you or your partner fit any of them.

- ☐ I can take care of myself on my own without assistance.
- ☐ I prefer to complete tasks by myself.
- ☐ I enjoy my space.
- ☐ I want people to leave me alone when they upset me.
- ☐ I frequently find myself unable to meet my partner's needs.
- ☐ I am at my most relaxed when nobody else is around.
- ☐ I want a friend who would not be demanding.

3.4 Insecure Ambivalence

Let's now meet a different couple. Jordon and Kate had two young children and resided in a modest two-bedroom home in the suburbs. Jordon had a nine-to-five job, and Kat was a housewife.

"He's angry with me; he's angry with the kids; he's angry with his boss. It is like nothing we do is enough, and I am getting his temper tantrums all the time," Kate complained when they finally sought therapy for their issues.

Jordon believed Kate was ignoring the causes of his rage and distress. He grunted, groaned, and made shocked faces because he couldn't sit still and talk to her for more than a few seconds.

Jordon's anger issues were founded on his interactions with his initial caregivers. Jordon and Anne's uneasiness started before their current partnerships. In other words, even though they were unaware of it, they arrived at the table this way. There needed to be a sense of security or firmness in Jordon.

When it comes to romantic relationships, the insecure ambivalent is the one that upsets the peace by obsessing on feelings of fear, rage, and conflict over being close. They are still burdened by the injustices and injuries from the past, which prevents them from truly moving on.

If both participants are insecure and ambivalent, there may be even more strife—a constant tug of war as the partners alternately get close and far. Prepare yourself for high drama if you or your partner are insecure and ambivalent.

Jordon's ambivalence resulted from his need for connection and his fear. He experienced both desire and rejection in turn. He resisted feeling happy, hopeful, glad and soothed. He approached his partner closely, hoping to connect, but swiftly withdrew out of fear of being let down. His inward movement and subsequent withdrawal identify an insecure ambivalence.

Jordon genuinely could not comprehend why he became angry whenever he saw Kate again after some time apart. He was baffled by his response.

If your spouse is an insecure ambivalent, appreciate your partner's presence. This is the most effective technique to overcome childhood trauma and quickly transition from feeling cherished. You gain from it when it occurs as well.

Activity 8: Are You Hopeless?

Do you believe you, your partner, or both may be insecure or ambivalent? Check if the following shared statements apply to you or your partner:

> ☐ I care about other people more than I do about myself.
> ☐ I am always giving and giving, but receiving nothing in return.
> ☐ I enjoy interacting with people and talking to them.
> ☐ I need to talk to calm down if you upset me.
> ☐ My partner tends to be quite egotistical and self-absorbed.
> ☐ When I am with my friends, I am at my most at ease.
> ☐ Love affairs are eventually draining and discouraging. Nobody can be relied upon.

3.5 Getting Close to Your Partner

This book will help you build a more stable connection and escape your anxious attachment. You will become a pillar if you stay in a stable relationship long enough!

The following supporting ideas will help you:

First, know your partner using the examples from this chapter. Which type of relationship best fits your partner? Please refrain from using this typology as a weapon against one another, as I have stated. It can cause harm if misused, just like any vital tool. Use it in your relationship with compassion.

Second, our goal in committed partnerships is not to develop new personalities or change who we are. On the contrary, it is our responsibility to be authentically ourselves. We should not constantly feel embarrassed about who we are or act falsely. Instead, we can be authentic while feeling accountable to ourselves and others. We must support our spouse in being boldly themselves in the same way that we are unapologetically ourselves. We should give each other complete acceptance in this way.

Of course, being authentically yourself doesn't imply that we are careless or irresponsible about how other people act or that we may use this as a justification for misbehaving toward them. You should prioritize attending to your partner's demands and worries rather than being unashamed whenever their voices cause you pain. Remember that establishing a couple of bubbles enables partners to protect and secure each other. So, your mission must be to be completely unapologetic about who you are.

Third, avoid attempting to alter your mate. We can both declare that we never change and that we all change. Both are accurate. And for this reason, acceptance is so crucial. Over time, our attitudes, habits, and even our brains may and do change. However, from birth to death, the underlying wiring that develops throughout our first experiences remains with us.

Sometimes these modifications erase the memories of our past traumas and phobias. Nobody ever becomes fundamentally secure after experiencing anxiety, pressure, rejection, or the danger of desertion. I can assure you that it won't occur. Anyone may only progressively become more secure via acceptance, high regard, respect, commitment, support, and safety.

Activity 9: See Your Partner in Different Light

Get ready to see your partner in a different light. Follow the steps:

> 1. Make a formal commitment to always being accessible to each other. When an agreement has been established expressly, it is simpler to stick to it in the heat of the moment. So, write it down and tell your partner.

This also allows you to express any opposition, reservations, or concerns. Discuss how you feel about being bound to your relationship. Consider your fears and potential gains from keeping this tie in place. Think about approaches to any circumstances where you wanted to hold back.

You can influence your partner by saying things like, "I am always here for you, darling," "You can talk to me anytime," or "I am all yours, 24/7."

> 2. Together with your partner, create go-to signals. You and your spouse might find it helpful to have means to communicate when you need to talk, especially at first. You could value a signal that eases the transition to being completely available.

Not all signals need to be spoken. You can use particular looks or hand gestures to let your spouse know they have your complete attention. For instance, grabbing both of your partner's hands can signal that you must put everything else aside to concentrate.

You and your partner may have more considerable expectations of each other, but the rewards could also be more significant.

Think about how your current or future relationship may be better if you had a more stable form of attachment to foster a healthier method of relating in romantic relationships. You must remember that happiness does not require you to be the epitome of a solid connection.

Two absolute paths cross each other. The first path is recognizing your biases towards yourself. Increasing your awareness of your experiences and helping you react to them more tolerant and sympathetic will help you.

Second, you must start by looking at the outer world from a new perspective. Building a connection beyond biases is where you should start. If a partner is unavailable, you can form a relationship with another important person from your family or friend.

4.1 Recognize Your Biases Toward Yourself

You already know who you are; you don't need to constantly uncover new aspects of who you are. Self-doubt results when you lack confidence in crucial aspects of your identity, which is common in those anxiously attached persons. Additionally, the more deeply you identify with a personality trait, the more driven you are to view your activities through that lens and act in that manner.

When it comes to your attachment style, which is an essential aspect of how you interact with the outside world, it is especially crucial to have a specific perspective of yourself and others. Your brain "assists" you by mentally representing what you anticipate seeing in yourself and yourself based on your style. Whether your attachment-related notions are correct or adaptive, it only takes a minimal bit of evidence for you to persuade yourself that they are true.

Confirmation bias is the phrase psychologists use to describe people's propensity to seek evidence to support their opinions. Psychologists refer to this tendency as self-verification when individuals utilize it to support their preexisting beliefs about themselves (whether positive or negative).

It is challenging to overcome your tendency to self-validate and perceive your life through a confirmation bias. However, you can start the process by becoming aware of your qualities.

Learning to Have a Positive View of Yourself

It's often believed that you can change how you behave with others just by becoming aware of when you're validating yourself too much or engaging in confirmation bias, like being overly critical of yourself or having an exaggerated fear of rejection. And while this is partially true, it's important to recognize that these insights can sometimes be distressing or unsettling. You might feel anxious, struggle with considering different perspectives, or sense that something doesn't feel quite right. What's more, instead of challenging your existing biases, you may be more inclined to challenge these new, more positive observations.

If you have attachment-related anxiety, you may discover that you confirm that you are unworthy in the following ways:

You pay great attention to any indication that you are weak, dependent, or otherwise imperfect while downplaying or failing to acknowledge your excellent qualities.

- You then recall statements or actions made by your spouse that seem to verify your belief that you are insufficient or fundamentally flawed.
- In the meantime, you forget the times your partner complimented or supported you when you were going through a difficult moment.

However, if you can identify your prejudices, you will be more receptive to—and even look for—a more objective viewpoint. You will gradually start having a new perspective on yourself and your partner.

Activity 10: How Do You See Yourself?

If you feel unworthy of love, please respond to the questions below to better understand how you retain this belief. It is a critical step in ending the cycle. Finish it about your significant other and other close individuals in your life. When you are naturally conscious of these concerns as you go about your days, stop doing this activity.

Write out your responses as a means to focus and direct yourself because the need to self-verify can make it challenging.

What happened recently that made you feel you deserve love or, at the very least, caused you to reevaluate your belief that you are unlovable?

How did it make you feel? (For example, content, uncomfortable, perplexed, or nothing.)

What acts of kindness or goodness did you perform today?

How have your loved ones, friends, or even random strangers shown you how much they care?

If you believe someone has made you feel unlovable somehow, are you possibly misinterpreting their purpose or intentions?

Keep in mind how you self-verify in each of these situations. What patterns do you notice?

4.2 Recognize Your Biases Towards Your Partner

When you've been conditioned to believe that others won't be there to support you, you may start seeing your partner as emotionally unavailable. This can lead you to feel like you're essentially alone, and as a defense mechanism, you may try to become more independent. When you question your own ability to receive love, you may start expecting that even those who seem accessible will eventually reject you.

As a result, even if you initially had positive opinions about your partner, you may start looking for signs that they're not really there for you, and interpret their actions negatively. For example, instead of considering that they might be busy at work, you might assume that they don't care about you if they don't contact you from work one day, or even suspect that they have ulterior motives to manipulate your emotions. This tendency to interpret things in a negative light is more likely to happen when you're feeling anxious and overly attached to your partner. These biases are influenced by your preconceived belief that your partner is emotionally unavailable, and it can be challenging to recognize this pattern of thinking.

Activity 11: Identifying Your Patterns of Communication

Paying attention to the communication patterns in your relationship, especially those connected to problems, can be highly illuminating. Important insights can be gained by keeping track of each partner's thoughts, feelings, and actions. Think about the following instance:

> *Tom was failed to spend time with April on the weekends. She believed that he was indifferent. She cried and told him he was selfish to convey this. Tom felt insulted and believed she was overly dramatic and withdrew in response. April had emotional pain, and the cycle continued.*

Consider a disagreement in your relationship that frequently recurs in light of this. Now think about the ensuing inquiries about it.

What do you think of what's going on? What were you contemplating for your partner?

What emotions do you think your partner was experiencing as a result? What was your spouse contemplating regarding you? What response did your companion give?

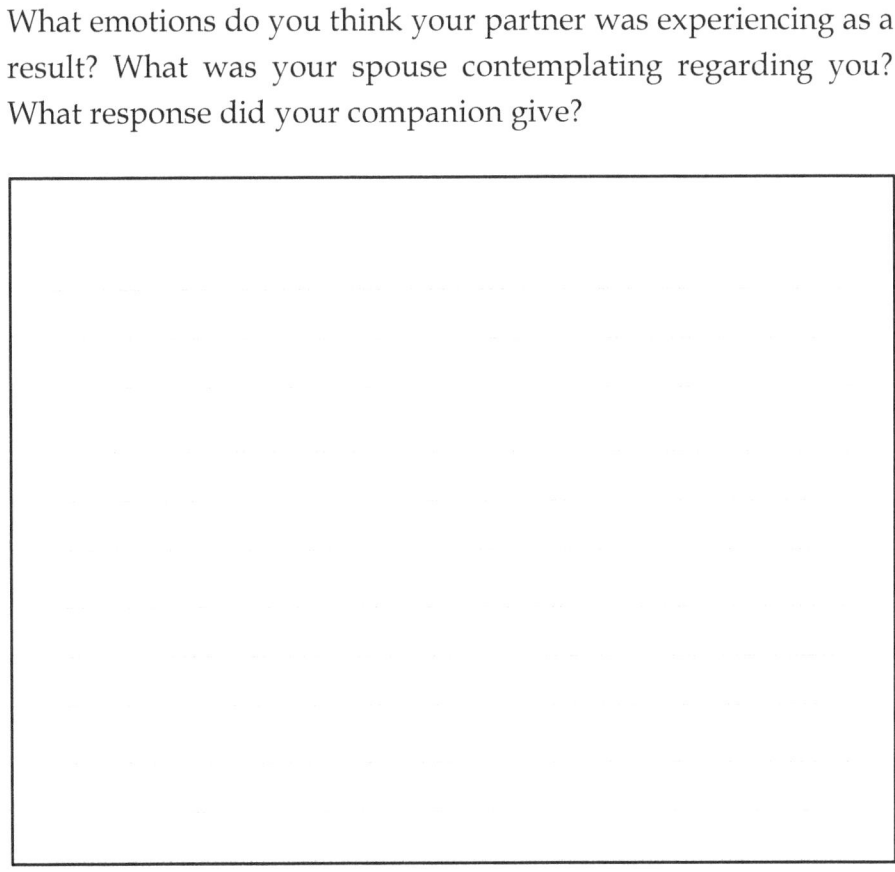

Take note of how the conversation develops and how it ends. Asking your spouse about their feelings and thoughts might be beneficial for answering questions about his experience, but only if you can have an effective conversation with them. If not, try empathizing with them and imagining their reactions, or get assistance from a reliable source.

How did this issue support your perceptions about your partner's emotional openness?

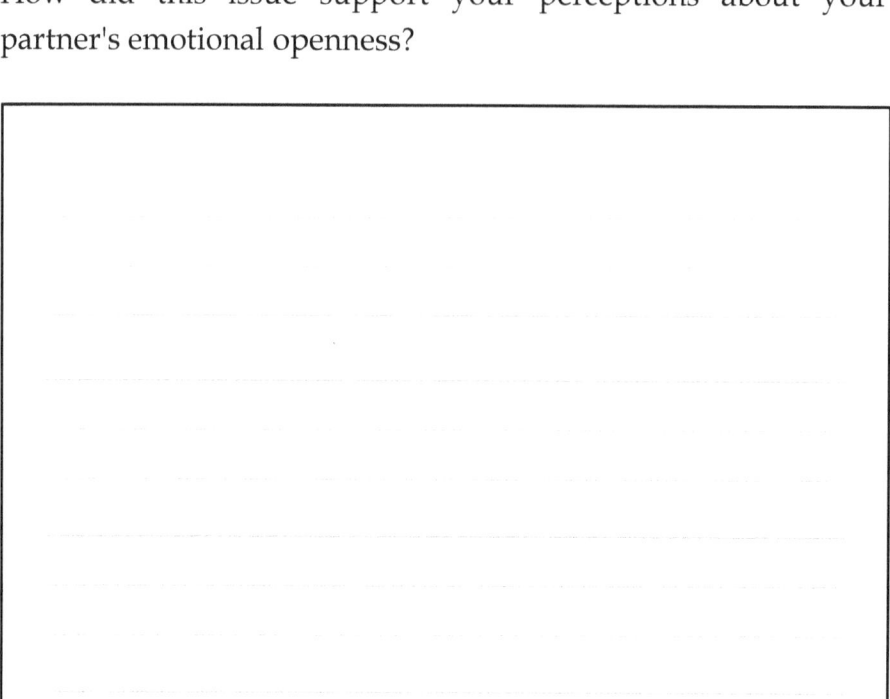

You should discuss this exercise with your partner and the insights it has given you at a suitable, calm time. You should also inquire about your partner's perceptions of your emotional openness and how the encounters affect their feeling of your deserving of love.

Chapter 5: A Path to a Strong and Secure Relationship

By now, you understand what drives you to maintain unhealthy and inefficient ways of your relationship with your spouse. You will continue seeing yourself, your spouse, and your relationship as always. But if you keep going, a fresh viewpoint will win. You will have more freedom to discover how to cultivate a fulfilling relationship and perhaps even alter your attachment style.

This raises a lot of hope, but the real challenge is figuring out how to maintain awareness of destructive patterns while fostering a fulfilling relationship.

Two ways exist to find relationship happiness and even "earn" secure attachment. A loving attachment figure is one way to make yourself emotionally available. It could be anyone you feel comfortable turning to for support.

The alternative route is what I refer to as compassionate self-awareness — being aware of yourself while also caring about and wanting to lessen your suffering. In both situations, love slowly seeps in to reassure you that you deserve it.

Compassionate self-awareness can aid in increasing your receptivity to a truly loving partner. Its two essential components are self-awareness and self-compassion, which I will go into more detail in this chapter. I will then give you in-depth exercises for developing each component of this crucial skill set.

5.1 Develop Self-Awareness

If you want to enhance your intimate relationships, you must examine your part in causing issues — or what prevents your relationships from starting. However, as I've already shown, people's biases often prevent them from seeing these truths. Making use of self-awareness effectively can therefore be challenging.

You will start to see more readily and clearly if you keep studying your propensity to confirm your beliefs of yourself and your spouse (or future mate). You won't take impressions for ultimate reality anymore, providing you more freedom to make good decisions. It is helpful to see self-awareness as being made up of awareness of emotions.

> *Amelia feared leaving her husband or tolerating her unpleasant married life. She felt dissatisfied. After accepting this, she looked inward and saw her problem differently. She decided to be happy without him. Of course, she had the option to accept the circumstance, but even then, she adopted a different mindset, which allowed her to choose the best ways for her deliberately.*

Think about someone who is mourning the loss of a loved one. This person may lock down his emotions if he is afraid of or tries to ignore his sadness, which keeps him emotionally numb (but insulated from the pain) and prevents him from connecting deeply with others. A person who is more accepting of their loss is typically able to communicate it with compassion.

Activity 12: Identifying Your Emotions

Your emotions, thoughts, and behaviors can all give you hints about how you are feeling. So, keep an eye on them every day.

You can experience intense sadness when you consider how little worth you believe people place on you. It would be more realistic to describe your feelings in this situation as "worthless" or "pathetic" rather than "sad." These words communicate an emotional experience while also reflecting thoughts or judgments.

Identifying Your Emotions

Fill this chart. It can be beneficial to do this at set times. You could also discuss them with your partner or a reliable friend. Use it to identify your emotions or how did you act in a particular scenario.

1.Date	
2.Situation (When you are upset, write down the circumstances.)	
3.Sensations (Write about your body's sensations.)	
4. Behaviors (Take note of your actions.)	

Do certain emotions surface as you focus on your feelings, actions, and thoughts? Try letting the feelings rise rather than trying to push a label of what you "should" be experiencing. You may put down "Frustration, hurt, and betrayal," for example.

This is crucial for knowing yourself, properly managing your emotions, and effective communication so that your partner can comprehend and, ideally, feel a connection with you. Therefore, it is highly recommended that you do this exercise, especially if you have trouble recognizing your emotions.

Activity 13: Naming Your Emotions

The process of naming and identifying your emotions is intertwined. To be able to interpret your experiences, you must take a certain amount of distance from them. Even for a while, this break away from your emotions helps you feel less immersed in them. Think about your current state of emotion to better comprehend.

Take note of how your thoughts after paying attention to them. Changing your focus to experience your emotions without becoming overwhelmed can be beneficial, especially when those emotions are powerful. Low-intensity emotions are less likely to overwhelm you.

> - Make it a habit to stop and think about your emotions at various points during the day.
> - You may do it, for instance, throughout meals, right before you leave the house, or as soon as you get to work.
> - Make a daily journal and write everything.

The key is to develop the ability to control how you experience your emotions by increasing your awareness and deliberately watching them. You will get more adept at doing this with stronger emotions with practice. And the more proficient you become at it, the more freedom you will have to observe your circumstance objectively—and possibly contemplate other explanations for or responses to it.

Activity 14: Embracing Your Emotions

You can focus on being more accepting of your emotions and making peace with them as you learn to tolerate them. You can start the process by focusing on particular emotional circumstances and taking the following into account:

Do your emotions improve the comprehension of your relationship with others?

Do your emotions indicate that you need to take care of a problem?

Do your emotions help you connect with your partner, and do they indicate empathy?

Even though they are challenging, emotions are a standard component of being a human. The ability to befriend them can be a long-term effort that you will need to practice for the rest of your life. Therefore, it helps to have patience with yourself.

5.2 Be Aware of Your Thoughts

Your thoughts impact how you feel about yourself and your beliefs. For instance, when you repeat ideas like "Andy doesn't love me," you feed self-doubt and low self-esteem. These ideas also elicit feelings of melancholy and rejection anxiety.

Learning how you maintain discontent in yourself and your relationship can be significantly aided in gaining consciousness. Having that awareness gives you a chance to work toward change. Sometimes the ability to be aware is all needed to bring about change.

Activity 15: Exploring Your Thoughts

This easy activity provides a potent illustration of how your thoughts impact you on various levels. Locate a peaceful area to finish it. It will only take a short while.

- Take a few deep breaths while sitting comfortably, then close your eyes.
- Slowly go from the bottom of your feet to the head. Recognize any sensations you may be experiencing, including any breathing or heartbeat sensations or tense muscles.
- Think of a criticism you have of yourself. Select the one that causes you the most trouble. Keep it in your head and say it aloud.
- Think about how this impacts you. What feelings do you have? What impact does it have on your feelings and thoughts?

If you dwell on your unfavorable self-perceptions, you might feel worse. You might feel your stomach churning or your chest getting tighter.

Repeat this practice but in a slightly different way.

Consider a time when you felt confident in yourself before you start. What kind of positive self-talk did you have?

```



```

As you finish this exercise, keep these ideas in mind. This will be more challenging if you are self-critical or hesitant to recognize your favorable attributes. However, as you do it, you will experience more good things, including more relaxed muscles and perhaps even more good thoughts.

Activity 16: Burst Your Bubble

Your negative ideas, whether they take the form of self-criticisms or beliefs, feed the uneasiness you experience because of your attachment style. Complete this activity to immediately alter these thoughts.

It is crucial to be patient with yourself, just like with so many other things I've discussed. It will take time to build a new way to feel because you are attempting to shift a way of being that has been a part of you since childhood. Take your time studying the chart. Write about it in your journal. Think about it until you are aware of the causing issues for you, as well as how it has affected you and your relationships in the past.

Date, situation, attachment-related anxious thoughts (about you and your spouse), effects on behaviors and emotions, and disconfirming evidence are the five columns that should be labeled.

Date: If you do this over several days, note the pattern.

Situation: Describe the specifics of the circumstance involving your present, former, or prospective spouse that made you angry.

Anxious/Negative thoughts: What thoughts feed your fear about attachment?

Effects on Behaviors and Emotions: Once you know what you are saying to yourself, consider how it makes you feel and affects your actions. For instance, constantly worrying that your partner will break up with you makes you likely to experience chronic anxiety, easily aroused jealousy, and possessive behavior.

There is no winning in this scenario. You won't notice this if he is genuinely dedicated to the relationship, and you will be disappointed. If he isn't devoted, you can hang on to the relationship out of a desperate need to win his appreciation.

Disconfirming Evidence: Pay attention to how your anxious thoughts result from your faulty thinking rather than the probable reality of your circumstance.

However, consider taking the opposing side yourself. For instance, if you are concerned that your boyfriend's outings with his friend indicate that he is not very interested in you, you might think about these questions:

What proof do you have that he is content with you? (For instance, he texts or calls you every day)

You need "a shadow of a doubt" so that you can use it as justification for evaluating different perspectives on yourself and your relationship. If your negative opinions of your partner are unquestionably genuine, it might be time to talk to them. You will gain from adding self-compassion to your growing self-awareness if you cannot behave in either of these ways or have no reasonable doubt about your unfavorable self-perceptions.

As you continue to fill out the chart, you may adopt a more optimistic viewpoint about your thinking. Decide to concentrate on the more uplifting and practical perspectives on your circumstance.

5.3 Building Self-Compassion

Self-awareness is a potent tool, yet it cannot solve your problems alone. Let's examine the other component of the equation for successful, long-lasting change: self-compassion.

It comes naturally for people to be kind to themselves and to relate with self-compassion after they embrace who they are and learn to befriend their emotions. Although individuals rarely discuss self-compassion, they frequently discuss compassion, which is the feeling of sympathy for another person who is suffering. It entails considering another person's viewpoint, demonstrating empathy, and wishing to lessen their pain. Simply adopting the same perspective toward yourself is self-compassion.

Activity 17: Where do You Stand?

Where Do You Stand?

It might be beneficial to evaluate your level of self-compassion. To determine your final ranking for the region, count the checkmarks. The more statements that apply to you, the more self-compassion you have. These statements will also guide you regarding what you must do to develop self-compassion.

- ☐ Regarding your flaws or deficiencies, you are forgiving and kind to yourself.

- ☐ When you make mistakes, you forgive yourself and treat yourself with kindness.

- ☐ When you are in pain or emotionally distraught, you care for and nurture yourself.

- ☐ To be happy in the long run, you should take good care of yourself.

- ☐ When you are in pain or emotionally distraught, you care for and nurture yourself.

- ☐ You assume that others share the same flaws or deficiencies as you do.

- ☐ Remember that others occasionally have similar challenges and emotions when you are sad.

- ☐ You will feel less alone if you remember that others occasionally experience similar problems and emotions.

- ☐ Even when you are upset, you may accept your ideas and feelings without passing judgment

- ☐ To embrace them, you must not deny, repress, or exaggerate your emotions.

- ☐ You try to keep a positive attitude even while angry or facing difficult circumstances.

Chapter 6: Become a Mindful Person

Being mindful involves being aware of your present experience while fully accepting it; maintaining this viewpoint gives you a sense of security, much like an attentive and accepting parent gives their child a sense of security, particularly during trying times. Mindfulness can help you create this mental image, just as a comfortable child can figuratively carry his emotionally accessible parent.

Mindfulness can strengthen your relationship by enabling you to react to your partner more confidently. You can remain anchored in the here and now while also being able to view your perspective, preventing you from getting sucked into a cascade of ideas and feelings associated with your concerns.

6.1 Living a Mindful Life

Mindfulness can reduce stress, emotional reactivity, rumination, increase focus, cognitive thinking, compassion, and decrease depression.

You can decide to meditate, which involves explicitly setting aside some time. This time can be for ten, twenty minutes, or even an hour, one or more times a day. Many people believe they can't meditate because they have trouble focusing or get restless while they're still. This lies in a misconception, though.

You don't need to restrain your thoughts or make them stay still; neither do you require a calm head. Instead, mindfulness meditation entails being fully present at the moment, distractions and all. The exercises that are provided below can help you learn some mindfulness fundamentals.

Activity 18: Mindful Breathing

Breathing is as natural as it gets. It takes place while you are doing, feeling, and generally preoccupied with the "contents" of your life.

- Close your eyes to breathe attentively.
- After that, focus on your breathing. Follow the natural course of your inhalation to the conclusion.
- Take note of the pause there. Then watch you exhale all the way through.
- With each breath, your tummy or chest rises and falls.
- Just remain conscious of the sensations you are experiencing.

Work on your consciousness every day with just one or two breaths. You can also plan to perform it once or twice a day as a meditation, spending fifteen to twenty minutes sitting or resting comfortably. Like working out, it is vital to begin cautiously and build up to your chosen practice; otherwise, you might need help to stop.

Activity 19: Mindful Walk

You can practice mindfulness and be aware of your breathing by concentrating on your physical sensations.

- Decide to walk thoughtfully, which is frequently done as formal meditation.
- You will benefit more if you do it for 10 minutes or longer.

- Spend time focusing on your body and genuinely feeling where it is. Recognize your purpose to be mindful.
- Feel your body shifting weight on your feet.
- Keep track of your distractions. Acknowledge to yourself that other thoughts are diverting you.
- Refocus on the walking sensations.

As you perform this exercise, be mindful of how amazing it is that you can walk and your body can support you. Be grateful that you can walk because not everyone can.

6.2 Feed Your Body and Soul

Self-compassion refers to treating oneself with care, as was covered in Chapter 5. It entails desiring what is long-term best for you. It is a significant driving force behind keeping up a healthy lifestyle.

The different methods of doing it are listed below.

People who experience anxious attachment are frequently too eager to stop taking care of themselves in favor of attempting to win others' love by taking care of them. While being kind to others is admirable, you harm yourself when you neglect taking care of your own physical needs.

Decide to prioritize maintaining a:

- Healthy diet
- Getting enough sleep
- Exercising frequently

By taking care for yourself this way, you cultivate the physical and emotional fortitude needed to appreciate life and successfully meet obstacles.

You need to deal with events beyond your control, overwhelming events (like your long-term girlfriend leaving you), and the apparent randomness of life.

There are various ways to cultivate this skill, including prayer, meditation, communing with nature, learning compassion and love, and performing good deeds. You might also attempt to live in harmony with the cosmos because you believe everything, including you, is interconnected.

Activity 20: Healthy Coping Ways

Life can be difficult. Sometimes all you want is some solace. Unfortunately, far too many people turn to unhealthy habits like emotional eating, withdrawing from others, drinking, buying, or gambling in an attempt to find consolation.

Adopt suitable coping mechanisms that, at the very least, occasionally work for you to point you in the right direction.

Make a list.

- Taking a stroll.
- Working out at the gym.
- Visiting the friends.
- Watching a movie.
- Reading
- Praying
- Practicing meditation
- Listening to music

These are a few examples of activities you may list. Put this list somewhere you can easily reach it so you may consult it whenever you need to. But if your troublesome coping strategies have you stuck, get expert assistance.

Activity 21: A Gratitude Journal

According to research, keeping a thankfulness notebook in which one lists things for which they are grateful makes people happier and more appreciative. Some studies say that you should do it every day, while others say once a week is preferable. Discover the frequency that works best for you.

I've found that people who have kept gratitude journals frequently behave consistently. They got the most out of it when they did it every day for eight weeks. They frequently struggled at first to even come up with something to be thankful for.

Activity 22: My Valuable Friends

Concentrate on the people you share interests with if you want to start making friends quickly. Get active in clubs or classes to further your interests. Finding hobbies that allow you to interact with people frequently is beneficial. Then, express interest in them or the others in your immediate vicinity. Be open to doing activities together as a friendship grows.

Then make a chart with the following headings:

My Friends: Under this heading, list your pals. You can include your closest childhood friend and a more recent acquaintance on your list of people who cherish you.

Valued Qualities in Me: List the qualities you believe these friends admire in you. Write down adjectives they would use to describe you, such as considerate, giving, honest, humorous, appreciative of the same things you do, helpful, offering sound advice, or a good listener.

Think about the traits you cherish the most. Each quality should be read and given time to sink in. Permit yourself to enjoy your sense of value and appreciation. It is acceptable if you catch yourself downplaying or disregarding these things. Like your eyes need time to adjust to light, you may need time to accept them. It could be beneficial to become used to viewing yourself through the eyes of your pals.

Keep this list at a location that is simple to find. Review it frequently. Remind yourself frequently that you are valued and deserving of love.

Chapter 7: Nurturing a Healthy and Supportive Relationship

Couples dancing together can be a lot of fun to see. Watching two people move in sync with each other is interesting. The most successful partners appear to be drawn together by some magnetic pull. Observing them dance allows one to experience being completely connected to another person. What is more alluring than that?

After finding a significant other, you should work to maintain a bond that, at its best, can resemble a flawless dance.

This way, you would get along well, communicate clearly, and ultimately trust each other. You would also be in sync with each other and with yourselves. Even in the worst-case scenario, you would still want a coordinated effort. The benefit of being in such a secure relationship is that it makes you feel safer both in your relationship and inside yourself.

7.1 Setting Relationship Goals

You need to be clear about your goals to reduce your relationship anxiety. Even if it is possible to meet someone great by accident, it helps to know what you want. This clarity can help you get started and lead the way to the right path.

In general, what contributes to a stable attachment during childhood also contributes to a secure relationship as an adult. We discussed them earlier in the book, i.e., a secure base and a safe place. Healthy relationships are those where the parties support and encourage each other's efforts.

Remember that both parties must develop these traits cooperatively as you consider them. To be emotionally available, partners must be open to accepting and being accepted, comforting and uplifting, which guarantees a safe haven in times of distress. It makes the relationship a stable basis from which to explore the world. Your partner must be able to accept them because an open give-and-take scenario fosters partnership. It is equally important that you can give and receive these things.

Activity 23: What Do You Want from a Partner?

Make a list to help you with this activity. Include every trait of your partner you can think of, such as personality, manner of relating to others, manner of relating to you, information about parenting (such as the desire to be a parent, desired number of children, or beliefs regarding each parent's role), occupation, physical attributes, and lifestyle.

You are unlikely ever to meet someone who meets all of your requirements. You will, however, have a greater chance of determining if that relationship is a suitable fit if you engage in this exercise.

7.2 Enhance Your Intimacy

Your initial encounters with your partner lay the groundwork for how the narrative of your relationship will develop. It will go more smoothly initially if you simultaneously open out to each other.

When one of you discloses something personal, the other responds by demonstrating empathy, understanding, and a similar level of disclosure. You grow accustomed to each other's company as you enjoy these private moments.

Your yearning for a connection could make you feel too exposed to open up; as a result, you might choose to keep your distance and cut yourself off. Both scenarios run the danger of alienating your partner. Additionally, it prevents you from getting to know her and developing empathy for the other person.

Getting involved in activities that make you feel like you are a part of something greater than yourself may also help you feel less alone and isolated.

You may say, "I feel nervous about letting my guard down," for example. You can choose to focus your attention by deciding to withhold further discussion for the time being. You allow this potential partner to introduce herself or enquire further about you. She might remark, "I understand exactly how you feel... " She might also ask you, "What do you mean?" on the other hand. By doing this, you may influence how your partner responds to your disclosures and your developing sense of connection, which should result in feelings of affection.

Activity 24: Trusting Each Other

Consider what pursuits you could enjoy doing on your own. Imagine how liberating or exhilarating doing these things might be. Remember that this is only a thinking experiment if you are also conscious of experiencing anxiety. You are not required to do anything; you are merely building a list.

You could discover that talking with reassuring people or writing down your thoughts in a notebook will help eliminate your anxiety or uncertainty.

Talk to your lover when you are ready. Pay attention to his reaction when you suggest your list. If he gives you the go-ahead, pursue your interests, and then let him know how it is going and how much you value his encouragement. Encourage him to explain any hesitation he may have, and then weigh the benefits and drawbacks of you pursuing your hobbies. If his fears sound realistic, discuss options you both feel comfortable with.

Now, ask about his hobbies and pay attention to how pursuing them might make him feel, or, if he's already doing so, how it makes him feel now. Consider what it might be like to encourage your partner to pursue his passions.

Activity 25: Doing Things Together

Whether you are dating or already in a committed relationship, sexual attraction is crucial to maintaining your romance.

Bodily stimulation makes this attraction stronger. It is especially crucial to discover other, healthier methods of arousing sexual desire and enhancing romantic interest if attachment-related anxiety has historically been the driving force behind your attraction. Here are some ideas for doing things alone or with your spouse before going out. However, you need to make your list.

- Riding a bike
- Hiking
- Playing tennis
- Brisk walks
- Dancing
- Attending concerts
- Seeing movies
- Traveling to new locations

Participating in these enjoyable and physically stimulating activities might introduce you to a new world. You can be attracted to someone who also makes you feel emotionally safe instead of using your fear of rejection to fuel your desire.

Activity 26: Show Affection

Physical affection is about showing someone that you love them. It is possible to hold hands, hug, massage your partner's feet or shoulders, or even briefly and delicately stroke their back. Naturally, there is also making love.

Some people are more at ease with touch than others. You may start today if you and your partner rarely interact.

> - Hugging each other in the morning or evening is a common habit. (I am referring to a prolonged hug in which both people are drawn in, not a rapid clench-and-release.)
> - Alternatively, you two may attempt massaging each other's feet or backs.
> - Start by simply cuddling.

If, at first, you find this awkward, that's okay. With time and repetition, you will notice that the discomfort fades and is eventually replaced by a warm, comforting sensation.

Activity 27: Praise Your Partner

Both verbal and physical interaction can improve your relationship. You don't always need to be so emotional while complimenting someone. The simplest insights that show affection for your mate are frequently the nicest compliments.

- You might compliment your partner on their amazing cooking skills or patience as parents.
- The sincere "I love you" is another option.
- Establish a daily ritual of complimenting your mate at least once.
- Do this activity for at least one week.
- Tell each other how it feels to be praised.

Activity 28: Let Each Other Know

During the early stages of a relationship, being kind to each other frequently comes easy. You get roses from him. You acknowledge and honor exceptional events like birthdays or noteworthy accomplishments. However, couples frequently experience times when partners take each other for granted.

> - Make a list of what your partner could do to show you love. This might be something he now does or something you want him to do. Be specific. You may include things like sitting next to me when we watch TV, holding my hand while we stroll together, or going with me to a basketball game.
> - Discuss the benefits and drawbacks of sharing your lists. Share your emotions with the people you love and trust.
> - Read your respective lists aloud to allow the other partner to hear and analyze them.
> - Spend some time working through this conversation until you both feel at ease.
> - Switch roles so that the other person becomes the listener.
> - Review this activity after a week. Discuss your feelings and views regarding the activity.

Activity 29: Prepare Gratitude Journal

By recognizing and valuing the positive aspects of yourself and your relationship, you can improve your thankfulness. Follow the steps:

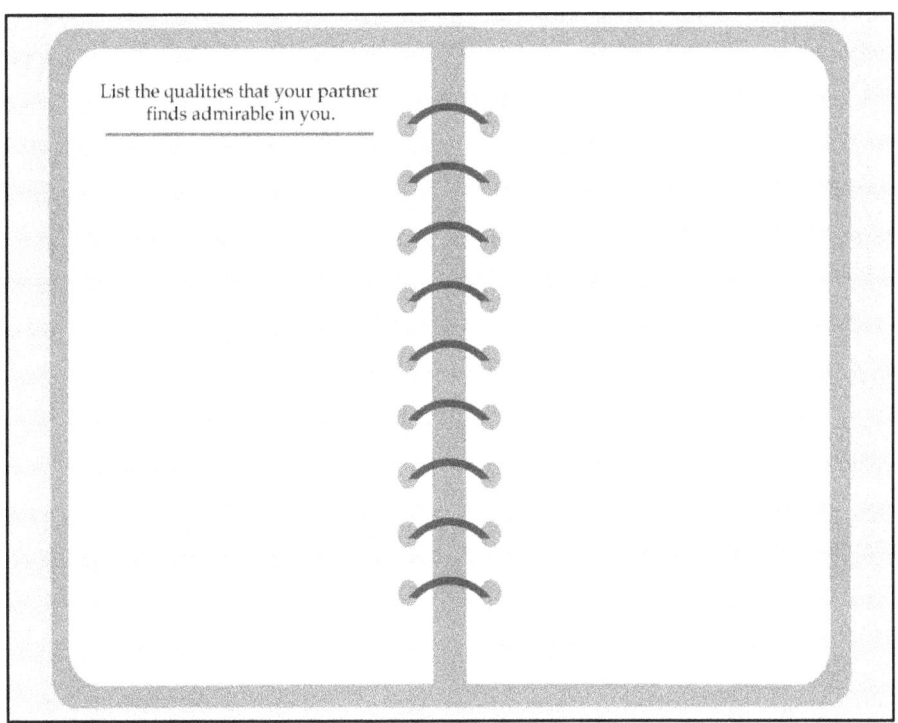

List the qualities that your partner finds admirable in you.

What are the qualities of your partner that are admirable and you find them attractive.

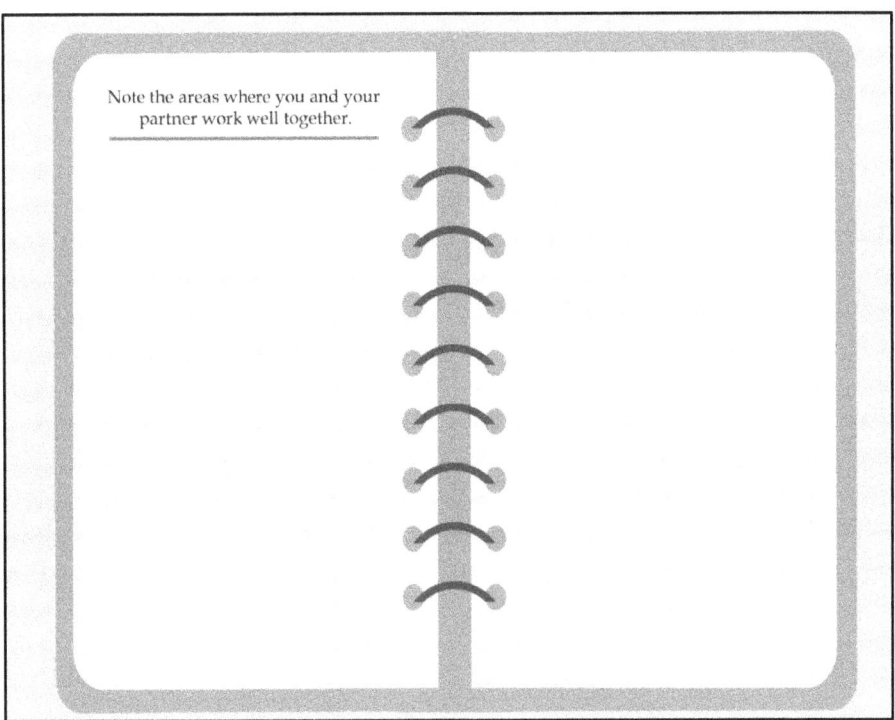

Note the areas where you and your partner work well together.

Accept, take in, and cherish every manner that makes your partnership a loving one.

Remember that only by making following these activities a regular part of your life will they likely yield meaningful and long-lasting outcomes.

Chapter 8: Handling Conflicts with Your Partner

All truly personal relationships have some misunderstanding, discord, or contention. However, if you tend to think about how you may win your partner's affection or attention and avoid rejection, you will probably go to great lengths to prevent such problems.

By developing compassionate self-awareness, you can learn to love yourself and accept your vulnerability. Additionally, you will be more receptive to compliments from kind people. Consequently, you will be more equipped to handle being open and honest with your spouse and paying attention to what they say without becoming distracted by how it may affect you.

You will be led step-by-step process of handling conflict in a helpful way in this chapter.

8.1 Be Open

Directly expressing your desires allows you and your spouse to collaborate in fostering your connection.

It might be helpful to concentrate on these two fundamental techniques:

---

1. Express your thoughts, desires, and requirements.

2. Be specific in your requests to your partner.

Activity 30: A Healthy Conversation

How you talk about a problem with your partner determines how the conversation will go. Choose a conflict and be cautious about how you strike up a conversation, and abide by these rules:

- Choose a moment to communicate that is emotionally neutral.
- Shortly describe the issue.
- Don't point the finger. Directly criticizing your partner's character flaws or going on about all the horrible things he has done will make him defensive.

When your partner upsets you, you may want to strike out at him or flee, but you want him to care and understand you. You must be completely honest about your feelings and thoughts for him to be able to do this.

Activity 31: Having Honest Conversations

Using "I" phrases is a typical strategy to accomplish this positively. By beginning a sentence with "I," you give your partner a glimpse into your life and let him into your universe. When you start a sentence with "you," on the other hand, you are criticizing your spouse and cutting off dialogue.

Consider the scenario when you and your partner talked about something you wanted them to stop doing—but they did. You could say, "I am angry with you for doing that. I feel unwanted. I feel so isolated. You are inconsiderate. I have no idea why I keep attempting to communicate with you."

The main goal is to be open about yourself so your spouse can truly "get" you and provide you with support, assurance, and value.

Talk to your partner once you are aware of your emotions and feelings.

You might remark, "I feel sad," or "I feel lonely," for example.

Tell your partner what they can do to fulfill your needs.

Talk it over with your spouse to devise a plan if you are unsure what they can do to make you feel better.

8.2 The Power of Effective Communication

Healthy communication necessitates communicating your thoughts, feelings, and goals, listening carefully to your spouse, and actually "getting" your partner—not just intellectually, but through empathizing with them and seeing things from their perspective. You need to be able to set your perspective aside to accomplish this. This strategy enables you to foster a sense of security in intimate and exposed interactions.

The power of effective communication lies not only in what you say but also in how you say it. Here are some pointers for good communication.

Ensure safety: Partners need to feel secure in their relationships. Only by concentrating on one person at a time during a conversation can this be fostered. When your partner raises a concern, make a sincere effort to comprehend his viewpoint.

Mirroring: What your partner says is a terrific technique to demonstrate that you "get" him. After he is finished speaking, repeat back in your own words what he has just said about his feelings. Say you need clarification and request more information.

See the Positives: When talking about a challenging subject, it can be helpful to occasionally point out qualities about your partner that you genuinely value.

Remain focused: Whatever the cause, problems never get solved while the focus keeps changing.

Be considerate: Intimate relationships depend on mutual respect. Thus, there is never a legitimate excuse to treat your partner disrespectfully.

Activity 32: Mirroring Exercise

Mirroring helps when you frequently feel that your partner is not hearing what you are saying. The "take-turn" method of mirroring involves one person at a time. When it is their turn to speak, the first person will describe their feelings.

- Choose a topic to talk about.
- Mutually decide who will speak first.
- Then change the turn.
- Use the techniques mentioned above to have effective communication.

Activity 33: Compassionate Listening

The 40-10-40 technique focuses primarily on effective conflict resolution and compassionate listening. Communication time is divided during this comprehensive form. Each participant receives 40% of the allowed time, with 10% to talk about their relationship.

Each speaker has their own allotted time to express themselves without interruption. The 40-10-40 procedure's crucial step makes sure no one makes accusatory accusations. This activity frequently leads to a fruitful discussion in which the participants acknowledge that, while the conflict in relationships cannot be avoided entirely, it is possible to survive it.

Activity 34: Make a Sandwich

The sandwich approach is one of the couple's communication activities that might prevent them from leaving anxious when asked for anything. You can "sandwich" your request between two affirmative statements rather than just making an outright demand.

For instance, consider starting your request with something like, "Thank you for listening to me. I need your help today. Can you pick the children up today from school? I recognize and value your time."

Make your sandwich and write down what you said to your partner.

Activity 35: Stress-Reducing Exercise

It is simple to absorb your partner's anxiety. If you want to fix your partner's problems every time they tell you, you may be exhausting both of you.

Stress-reducing dialogues are a type of communication exercise that allows the speaker to express their stressors while allowing the listener time to hear without responding. The participant in this activity listens without offering suggestions or attempting to discover a solution.

This should be done for 15 to 20 minutes at night time. Exercises in the stress-relieving discussion can strengthen your relationship and enhance your listening and communication abilities.

Activity 36: Forgiveness Sets Your Free

People should start forgiving by appreciating a time when they have already been forgiven.

Consider the reasons they might have pardoned you and how pardoning someone made you feel. Think about how it improved your relationship, your partner and you. Think about something in the past you are unable to forgive, then follow the steps given below:

- Use compassion and understanding.
- As you do, keep the upsetting occurrence in mind. This should enable you to view the issue and your partner's actions with more insight.

- The objective is to maintain your personal experience throughout this process while also being able to empathize with your spouse. Although it can be challenging, doing this is crucial.
- Practice switching back to the activities that help you connect with your personal experience and those that foster empathy for your partner to aid in the process.
- There are certainly occasions when you feel compelled to revisit the earlier hurt and rage. You will have to reason with yourself to overcome them.
- Respond with self-compassion when the offensive behavior crosses your mind.
- Try to focus on the now.
- Focus on the love your partner currently shows you.

Activity 37: Making the Hard Choice

Creating a strategy that will enable you to walk away from your relationship if it is beyond repair is critical. So, follow the steps:

- Create a network of support in advance.
- Accept your grief. Feel the sorrow, rage, hurt, or anything else you are feeling.
- Keep in mind your worth and your best qualities.
- Pick sane strategies for coping. While taking care of yourself is a good idea no matter what, it becomes much more crucial during trying times.
- Work on something worthwhile.
- Remain present in the now.

Be ready for the want to reconnect. You will likely consider returning to your lover at some point in the future. Do a reality check if your mind is overflowing with pleasant memories and answer the following question.

Did your relationship have fun moments in your relationship?

Examine your motives for leaving.

Write at least three reasons to take an exit from your anxious relationship.

Be kind to yourself if you decide to turn around.

Breakups are never simple, but knowing what you want gives you a greater chance for a stronger, more stable relationship.

Final Thoughts

"Life of Anxiously Attached Couples" weaves a story of love, vulnerability, and self-discovery that sends readers on an emotional rollercoaster. The book deftly examines the intricacies of interpersonal relationships through the compelling tale of two individuals battling their deep-seated worries.

This book penetrates expertly into the protagonists' psyche, genuinely portraying their most private thoughts and anxieties.

Readers are taken into a realm of self-reflection and urged to consider their attachment styles and emotional trajectories. They are encouraged to examine their weaknesses and face their concerns by using the book as a mirror.

Ultimately, this book is a compelling story about the highs and lows of love. It is proof of the complexity of interpersonal interactions, the value of self-awareness, and the therapeutic potential of meaningful, sincere, and secure connections. This book will provide readers with anxious attachment a renewed awareness of the complexities of love and how we relate to others.

www.ingramcontent.com/pod-product-compliance
Lightning Source LLC
Chambersburg PA
CBHW051218120626
46547CB00013B/1407

*9 7 8 1 9 6 0 0 2 0 9 1 8 *